Baltimore Girls

poems by

Lynne Viti

Finishing Line Press
Georgetown, Kentucky

Baltimore Girls

For Jill,
with love
and thanks,

Lynne

March 2017

ACKNOWLEDGMENTS

The author wishes to acknowledge the editors of the following publications in
which these poems first appeared:

The Basil O'Flaherty, "Baltimore Girls"
BlazeVOX, "Making Love to You Was Like Peeling"
Callinectes Sapidus, "Crabbing on Isle of Wight Bay"
Foliate Oak Literary Magazine, "Diva," "Judgment," "Preparations"
Grey Sparrow Journal, "Engineer"
In-flight Literary Magazine, "Suze in Midsummer"
The Little Patuxent Review, "I Learned That Marilyn Had Died"
The LongLeaf Pine, "Girl, With Eyelash Curler"
Meat for Tea: The Valley Review, "Brantwood Lane Miscellany"
A New Ulster, "Inclined Plane, Pulley, Wheel & Axle," "Early Morning in
Kresson," "Salad Days"
Paterson Review, "Pâtissière"
The Song Is…, "I Can't Get No"
Subterranean Blue Poetry, "Shades at the Reunion," " Nickel Dreams"
Work to a Calm, "Burn Your Darlings"

Publisher: Leah Maines

Editor: Christen Kincaid

Cover Art: Gay White

Author Photo: Thomas Viti

Cover Design: Barbara Aronica Buck

Printed in the USA on acid-free paper.
Order online: www.finishinglinepress.com
                also available on amazon.com

Author inquiries and mail orders:
Finishing Line Press
P. O. Box 1626
Georgetown, Kentucky 40324
U. S. A.

Table of Contents

For the Baltimore girls: Chris, Debbie, Francine, and Gay

Salad Days

We lived at home, were always home
for dinner. We thought we dressed like women, but only
when we peeled off the school uniforms and slid into
plaid kilts, blouses with Peter Pan collars and circle pins,
loafers, on Friday night, for a church hall dance.
We thought we knew everything, though we only
knew everything about the things we read in books
or heard on the bus, or on the street. We read
magazines to learn how to flirt.
Being sophisticated meant smoking Benson and Hedges,
we wondered how old we'd have to be
to drink at a cousin's wedding.

Our mothers thought our world was crazy.
Too much Orbison and Presley, then in a whirr,
James Brown, the man in the orange cape, and
the Beatles, who made us scream, or the
Subversive Dylan, who questioned us,
How does it feel, to be on your own?
—when our mothers wanted us to be safe.
Take the bus to school, be home on time.
No drinking, no smoking, study hard,
Go to college. Find a nice boy. Get
married, stay in town. Our town, which
changed and burned, changed and burned again.
Some of us left, and those who
Stayed didn't always follow the playbook.
We are neither who we were when we were sixteen
Nor are we different from who we were, inside,
even though we've tried like crazy to: speak up,
grow up, let go, not judge, relax, achieve, kick back,
question, breathe, believe, not believe—

Now we size ourselves up
against the dreams and goals and fantasies
we had as girls, the plans we spoke of,
the ones we hid. Back then, we didn't say
It's all good, but it is. The whole journey,
The paths and detours, all good, all worth
something, the living of it, the becoming,
never stepping into the same river twice.

Early Morning in Kresson

In my mind's eye I see it—the stub of a macadam road
dead-ending into Blue Diamond Coal, its trucks
lined up each morning for the long hauls.
To the left, the junkyard, heaps of metal and rubber, hard by
an Italianate house, rust-brown, coated with years
of dust and cinder ash, facing the junkyard cranes instead
of a lawn. A porch swing, always vacant even on summer
evenings. Only the metal cranes noticed.
The folks who lived in the house, white-haired, plainly dressed,
bespectacled, came and went together, but mostly stayed home.
My father's tavern sat amongst these places, the last
in a row of houses. In its former life, the bar
housed a bakery, we heard—the baker's family
lived upstairs in the cramped rooms, their kitchen
the bakery itself. I used to pretend I could smell
bread baking, the sweet fragrance of airy
white loaves turning golden in the long-gone ovens.

I went along with my father there before dawn,
the half-light bathing the block in sepia.
I sat at a small table in the back bar reading comics—
my father rolled kegs of beer up from the dank cellar.
Up on the ragged sidewalk I stood peering down
as he slid the keg into a handtruck, up a plywood
ramp, and into the tavern.
Light crept in through the glass bricks in the storefront.
I leaned around the corner of the darkwood bar,
watched him roll the keg from handcart to its station,
waited for the hiss when he tapped the silver barrel.

I inhaled the faint yeasty smell, which oddly, offended—
and pleased me. Sounds of traffic began to flow in
from the bar's back door, still propped open. I was
sent to pick up the paper from the doorstep, laid it
on my father's work table near the curved jukebox.
It wouldn't be switched on till lunchtime. Hank
Williams' and Jerry Lee's wails issued from it.
But by then I would be back home—quiet streets,
small green lawns, lolling on an old quilt spread in shade.

Engineer

He was the boy who loved trains
of all kinds, and trolleys—back
when they still ran along the roads to
Carney and Towson, all the way
to the route's end, Woodlawn or Windsor Hills
places I knew only as names
on placards, black print on white in
the front of those streetcars
or white on black on the turning
signage at the side of the car,
Irvington, Forest Park, each
mysterious terminus.

He was the boy who set up the Lionel
trains on the sheet of plywood
painted green to look like fields
trains that ran past a station, a school,
a town hall, fields with tiny metal
cows that grazed on painted wood.

He wore the motorman's hat
or the engineer's striped cap,
stacked glossy
train magazines on his bookshelf,
talked of nothing but steam locomotives,
electric trains, old straw-seated trolleys
bus routes through Baltimore
till his world expanded and he learned
the subway lines in New York and Boston,
discontinued private companies,
public utilities, anything so long
as there were cars carrying people
or empty cars late at night or in the
first run out of the car barn.

Car barn—when was the last time
someone said those words
or cared about car barns?

Now he's often confused, often
unsure of how to log into email, uncertain
which day it is or
where his wife goes
when she leaves the house.

Someone said the cops came one day,
he might've done something wrong.
They pushed him down
into the squad car
as he yelled, talk to my wife, please,
call my wife, she'll explain.

It's nothing like that, we later heard.
It's his mind, it's slipping,
He fears he can't remember things
won't remember the stops on the Number 19 line
won't remember where they built
the diesel-powered buses we rode to school,
their fumes sweet and nauseating all at once.

When we were young he let me throw the switch and
start the train running. Sometimes
he let me drop a pellet into the engine's smokestack
and gray smoke, pungent like incense, poured
out of the engine as it clicked along the tracks.
Sometimes he let me throw
the switch so the train turned off onto
a loop that led to the roundtable
where he did repairs, touched
up the paint here and there, let
the engine rest.

Heads together, we leaned
over the platform, the tracks,
in the train world he created.
Light slanted in through the basement window.
Look, he said, flicking on the red signal.
He slowed the train to a halt, pointed
to the coal car. We need more fuel, he said.
He threw the switch then. I thought
he was king of the railroads.

Inclined Plane, Pulley, Wheel & Axle
For Mary Jane

I studied the euthanasia coaster,
the Lithuanian artist's drawings, the steep
first stage of the steel thing, the sharp
drop meant to cause hypoxia to the brain,
seven inversion loops, clothoids
designed to drive passengers into brain death.

At the end of the ride, said the
artist, they would unload—Unload!—the bodies
then do it over again with
fresh comers.
Strange to think that
coasters that thrilled generations of
those four feet or taller
who climbed into the toboggans for a night of fun,
could be made into death machines,
for euphoric and elegant death, said the artist—
to solve the problems of life extension.
We used to call that long life.

We rode the old wooden coaster once.
When the bar was secured
We gripped it hard,
shrieked and screamed, which made it
all the more wonderful. My hair
blew out behind me and
my stomach
leaped up into my heart, which
jumped into my throat.

Your father came to the front door
for his weekly visit, his old car
parked in front of your handsome house.
We were off to Gwynn Oak Park with him—

your brother, you, and I. Did we ride
the Deep Dipper or the Little?
I dreaded both, but you said
your father would sit between us.
We'd be tucked in safe and we could
yell as loud as we liked.

The ascent scared me far more than
the fast drops towards earth. I hated the
creaking of the toboggan train as it
made its way to the crest.
But the plummeting was a joy,
then we curved around a bend and it
started again, the slow climb.
Three times I felt pure bliss,
heard a scream shoot out of my head.
Your father was solid between us,
he laughed and hooted. It was
the only time I ever saw him happy.

You were a brave girl. I was uncertain
about such things as roller coasters. You
stayed in Baltimore, married, had kids.
I left as fast as I could and kept moving.
You died before you were fifty, leaving me
to reconstruct my memories.

You wouldn't like this Lithuanian artist's notion,
his good-death coaster, the
24 passenger trip through euphoria to
quick death. Hearing him, you'd tug at
your blond hair, turn, walk
into the sunny afternoon, far
from the black toboggans.

Judgment

Two nights after
the president was shot
my mother went out.

She put on silver blue eyeshadow.
She wore her Persian lamb jacket
with the mink collar.
It was the year
she was having the kitchen redone.
The house was in disarray.

I sat on our brocade sofa.
I watched
the small black and white tv.
It sat in a temporary place
atop an end table.
I watched
the news replay
Jack Ruby shooting Oswald.

A boy I thought I liked came by.
I didn't like the way
he chugged from the green Coke bottle,
swished it around like mouthwash
before he swallowed.

I never forgave my mother.
I wanted her to sit
on the sofa with me
and cry.

Crabbing on Isle of Wight Bay

At an old footbridge we set up—
Tied the chunks of eel to twine, threw the lines
as far as we could, so the crabs
might think they'd chanced on a choice breakfast.

Pull the lines gently, my father said, draw
the string in slow and steady. We stayed for hours,
not much to do but test the lines, nibble sandwiches
a half at a time, drink grape soda from the can.
We gazed down at the current, saw
the lines drifting away from where we sat,
making parallel lines in the green water.

Throw him back, my father said, when
we netted a small one.
Too, there was his prohibition
against keeping the female,
her apron marked by deep ridges.
I turned the net inside out and let her go.

That night in the tiny cottage kitchen
we splashed beer and vinegar into the pot,
turned on the blue gas flame.
Barehanded, my father lifted the scuttling creatures
one by one from the cooler, dropped them into the pot.
We sprinkled the crabs with Old Bay.
I heard them moving about, rattling against one another, then
it was eerily quiet. The sweet, spicy smell
of crab suffused the room.
I breathed it in deeply.

We hammered away and picked,
praised backfin and clawmeat,
licked the seasoning from our lips.

Preparations

Don't kid yourself
into thinking that the past isn't still
stuck fast inside you, no matter how you will it
away or meditate until you think you touch
infinity, or the edges of it, if infinity
has edges, like the edges of the yellow walls
where they met
or the edges of the wooden window frames
in the room where you gladly gave up
your virginity, another thing
in your to-do list before college.

That longhaired girl with ivory skin
freckled in summer, body slimmed
by regimen of hardboiled eggs and grapefruit
—she's still with you. She stretched out
on the narrow bed, raised her arms
above her head, looked into the eyes
of her novice lover, the one
she chose for the deflowering,
as if she might find some clue,
some notion of how to be a woman.

And after, when the thing was done,
she was done with him as well.
It was more or less a
disappointment, an act
to have behind her.
When he left that day, she knew
only that one more line
could be crossed off her list.

The old steamer trunk her aunt had lent her
sat in the hallway, its drawers and shelves
waiting to be filled.

Diva

Stand up in front of your class
on a rainy day when everyone's done the seatwork,
with twenty minutes to kill before the bell.
Sing Secret Love or
Young and Foolish—unaccompanied.
Bother Mrs. Smith till she lets you sing a solo,
What Child Is This in the Christmas concert
in the gym, everyone in white shirts,
the boys in dark pants,
the girls in navy blue skirts,
yours is a cheap one
from Epstein's in Highlandtown
because your mother
says you'll only wear it once,
why spend more money?
Sing The Telephone Hour from Bye Bye Birdie
at the first assembly in your all-girls school,
Eight girls in summer uniforms, fists to ears
Crooning into imaginary handsets,
hi Penny, hi Helen, what's the story?
—on the stage that rises up
from the gym's polished floorboards.

Then the singing stops, at least in public.
Singing in the shower doesn't count, or
singing at rallies, ain't nobody goin to turn me round
where have all the flowers gone, one, two three,
what're we fightin for, don't ask me.
In the car on the way home from the play,
slaphappy and tired, sing the Marseillaise,
Sing show tunes, that was a real nice clambake.
At home, sing Surabaya Johnny along with Bette Midler
on the stereo, the last record on repeat, repeat.

When the babies come, sing old Beatle songs, sing Sinatra,
It happened in Monterey a long time ago, sing Girl Scout tunes,
I'm happy when I'm hiking, baby's boat's a silver moon,
sing Raffi, Rosenshontz, can you tell me how to get,
how to get to Sesame Street.

Now it's quiet in the house. Everyone's
out or has moved away. Leave the radio off,
keep the Ipod silent. Sing
whatever you please.

Nickel Dreams

Along the Fuller Brook path wending
through backyards, there's no one about
except a few women with
small dogs on leashes. The brook—
not as high as I expected.
The blackened piles of snow
all melted away, roof rakes,
ergonomic shovels, the chemicals
we strewed on sidewalk and porches.
Mere memories of winter.

The sun strains to appear.
It warms the day but I hardly
see my shadow, only faint
suggestions of a shadow, a darkening
across the path.
On a day like this, full of spring's promise,
I cut jonquils from my mother's garden
wrapped them in newspaper, a cone
around the butter yellow blooms.

Go to 30th Street Station, Mike said, for the transfer
But watch out if you're there right at six, when
the hounds are let off their leashes,
dogs in gray flannel suits, carrying
smart leather briefcases. I understood.
He loved to quote Dylan: *I don't want to be*
a singer in the rat race choir.

As I rose near my stop on the Paoli local
an old man glanced at my flowers.
I withdrew one and handed it to him,
without a word, hopped off at Haverford.
Mike stood on the platform, his long scarf

artfully draped around his neck,
tweed sport coat festooned
with buttons of Lenin, Freedom Now, Stokely
Carmichael. We walked through the campus,
his arm around my shoulder.

This will be my life, I thought.
His roommates were out. We
skipped dinner, built a fire. We
talked about the war, about Yeats.
When it was late and
we were so hungry we couldn't stand it
we strolled to the Blue Comet
for cheeseburgers—I remember
even now how good they tasted.
We walked the back way to the women's college
—I'd set up camp in the guest lounge.
Mike kissed my cheek, handed me a nickel
the Paoli local had flattened into an oval,
Washington's head all distorted.
I carried it around for years,
that talisman of my life to come.

I Can't Get No

Satisfaction, we danced in the basement to the Stones.
Your mother introduced us to her boyfriend.
They sat upstairs drinking iced tea.
The August night was humid,
the lightning bugs were already out dancing
across the wide lawns.
You'd survived a year of college.

I'd slimmed down, in preparation for it.
I grew my hair long.
pinned it up into a French chignon
trying to look like a girl in a Truffaut flick—
You were the only one who noticed.

No satisfaction, no satisfaction.
You danced with everyone at your party
Beach boys or Stones or Smokey
Robinson and his Miracles—

You kept your hair short, close
To your head. You still favored the
Madras shirts, khaki pants,
boat shoes, no socks, you were
the preppiest guy I knew.

I never saw anyone who
could dance like you, so abandoned,
it could be Mersey sound, blues beat, r&b.
You were an equal opportunity
music loving dance machine—

At midnight when I knew I had
To collect my girlfriend and get on home
Though I wanted to stay and dance on with you—
I threw my arms around you,

turned my cheek so my ear
Was up against your clavicle.
You were breathless, smelling of
Lark cigarettes and soap.

Call me tomorrow, you said.
I walked up the stairs to your mother's kitchen
I drove across the city in my father's Chevy
to my part of town.

My hair had come unpinned.
I slipped into my nightgown,
washed my face. I felt so lucky
you were my friend,
one who asked so little,
who made me laugh and shared
his cigarettes and his scotch with me
his fake cynicism and his jokes.

You were never my boyfriend,
never my lover. You were
the companion who years later
left me a poem
handwritten but rolled
into my old typewriter,
blue-black ink, corrasable bond.

Girl, with Eyelash Curler

The teacher left the room for five minutes
And with algebra book splayed open on the desk
You reached into your purse
And withdrew a Maybelline eyelash curler
A medieval cage contraption, only in miniature.

You artfully, dramatically
Manipulated your already-curly lashes.
With each squeeze of that instrument of beauty torture
you opened your other eye wide, peering over
at those near you. Who could resist
that fake look of surprise you'd mastered?
Who didn't envy those large anterior chambers,
blue eyes expressive, half-sad, half-joyful?

First, two or three of us near you noticed,
then in concentric circles
Your fandom grew till we were all
barely able to hold in laughter—
Some of it slipped out in giggles, then
just when we were all about to erupt
into rows of laughter—

Sister walked back into the room.
All was silent.
Heads down, we pretended to solve the equation.
You quickly slipped the eyelash curler
Into your handbag.
You kept a look of absolute seriousness on your face—
Seriousness belied by the devilish gleam of your eye.

Girl, you were so damn funny.

Baltimore Girls

We weren't the prettiest but
We knew how to pretty up.
We weren't the smartest but
We could hit the books.
We weren't the richest but
We knew how to make do.
We weren't the bravest but
We put on a good front.

We were in a hurry to get
Out of town, out of state,
Through school, to a job,
To a place of our own.
We had no time to waste on
Sitting still, feeling sorry for ourselves,
Crying more than a day over a boy.

—Those were the girls we were
Not exactly tough, but no hothouse flowers.

I'd love to sit down and have a smoke
With them, a Newport or a Winston,
Puff out perfect smoke rings.
I'd like to drink a couple beers with them
From a stash hidden in the weeds
Out near Loch Raven Dam.

How perfect to meet my old self.
We could tell each other such stories.

Shades at the Reunion

When we gather like this around the table,
every five or ten years
drinks in hand, raising toasts,
in the back of our minds, always, are the ghosts:
The cousin who died at forty, when the cancer flared.
The school friend, gone at barely fifty—she loved her smokes.
Toxins and her genes teamed up to do her in.
The rest of us—we've survived so far, though we're not sure why
or how. We dare not probe.

My friend the hard-edged newsman
laughed when he told me his on-air transition phrase
"elsewhere in the news"—as if we could
move from tsunami to oil spill to death of an ex-president
with any kind of grace. When he lay dying
in his hospital bed in Croton-on-Hudson
this old journalist stared at tv images of Baltimore burning.
It's all like it was before, he murmured.

Knowing all this, we sit in the cool air,
September sun on our faces,
hearing the songbirds carry on
like Yeats' miracles in Byzantium.

Brantwood Lane Miscellany

August to August, we made a little family.
The house was too big for us.
That year there was always a confluence of menses.
A stream of lovers, either too young or too old
sent by well intentioned matchmakers
passed through the door. None stayed long.

We were barely women then, more like girls:
One insomniac,
One losing her hearing,
One itching to go north to New Haven or Boston.

We came and went by the front door
turned away the Jehovah's Witnesses
shutting the door hard,
laughing nervously.

At night we drank scotch
or shared a joint.
Mornings, two of us drank coffee,
One wouldn't touch the stuff.
I cooked, Martha did the washing up.

Our mascara stained the white towels.
Our laughter annoyed the neighborhood.
When we left for good
the garden was just bearing fruit.
We missed out on that harvest.

Workdays, the AM morning all-news station
was pouring from the upstairs bedroom,
And sometimes one was
startled out of sleep at 3 a.m. by twin noises,
the vacuum and the stereo.

Pâtissière

The December you made a poundcake
your mother's fat cookbooks were stacked
all over the white kitchen.
The cupboards were so high you had
to stand on a wobbly stepladder.
I steadied it as you pulled down
the old china from Sauveterre.
It was painted with tiny roses and vines.
Plates just large enough for a fat slice
of buttery cake, dotted
with gold raisins and crushed pecans.

You couldn't have been more than fifteen.
That winter you made your way through
Craig Claiborne, James Beard, Julia Child.
I'd see you
chin resting in an open hand, elbow
on the white table, the other hand
flipping through stained pages.

That egg yolk yellow cake was just
the moister side of dry
but not dry, so solid
I made a meal of it. Have another,
you said, slicing through the thin brown top
into the golden mass of cake.
A pound of butter, you told me, a pound of flour,
a pound of extra fine sugar.
It's a recipe that's
almost not a recipe at all.

You went off to college, immersed
yourself in semiotics, found
a boyfriend, then later,
a husband, a divorce, then
a business partner, then two. You got
a love, a child, a flat that made its way
into the *Times* Home section.

There have been awards all these years
but not for cakes. There have been
honors, attestations, prizes. You're famous,
on panels, on juries, you're in Wikipedia!

Has there been no poundcake? No chipped china
from your grandmère? No recipe that's
not a recipe at all?

You wore small tortoise shell glasses. Your hair
needed a good cut. You wiped
your buttery hands on your flannel shirt
and scraped the last bit of batter from the bowl.
You licked your fingers, wrapped
dish towels around your hands,
Slid the cast-iron pan into the oven.

Come back in two hours, you told me,
we'll have cake for dinner tonight.

I Learned That Marilyn Had Died

Not Monroe but Marilyn the English teacher
Who befriended me the first day of my first job
Who invited me to her thirtieth birthday—
Marilyn the inveterate New Yorker
from West Virginia who lived
In a tiny studio apartment on the
Upper East Side when
Nobody could afford to live there.
Marilyn who taught me how to sew pantsuits
When it was radical to wear them to school.

Marilyn who had pale skin and black hair
A long face, a cutting word,
Who wouldn't let her students say, *This is boring,*
But made them say instead, *This did not reach me.*
Marilyn died who later slept with my ex after our breakup—
He can't remember this because
He never remembers anything he did before
The new millennium.

I lost touch with Marilyn after she met a man
on the train coming back from Lake George.
She called to tell me she was engaged to him,
warned me not to get involved with a younger man.
I ignored her, never saw her again.

She liked dogs, a special breed, I don't know which one.
She never married, became one of those beloved teachers
Everyone remembers forever—

Her father used to leave her and her kid brother
Locked in the car on his way home, he stopped at a bar.
He'd be in there for hours drinking—
I'd never heard of a Jewish alcoholic
Or even Jews in West Virginia
She said they weren't observant,
never went to temple, no bat mitzvah.

She loved the theater, the students, the Upper East Side,
Expensive scotch, fine restaurants in midtown, and the beach.
She loved Gatsby, Hamlet, Sylvia Plath, Melville,
Anne Sexton, John Donne.
She wore a doleful look, even when she smiled,
She had black lashes against white skin.
Her dark wit made me laugh and wonder
Really, what was so funny about what
Was so sad. I wish I knew
What became of her, before
Her short ticket was punched.

Making Love to You Was Like Peeling

Making love to you was like peeling
An onion. I teared up, holding the knife's edge
Against paper-thin layers, pulled them
Away, one by one by one. I knew I must
Get to the tender parts of you, underneath.

Making love to you was like scraping
The hairy root vegetables, bright carrots,
The pale parsnips, the knife blade flat
Against the tubers—I needed strong hands
To hold you, to interlace my fingers with yours
To show you how desperate I was.

At night, after sex, I should have been exhausted
But I heard you turn on the shower, call
To me to join you. Afterward, I enfolded you in
A rose-colored towel big enough for two.
It was like rinsing tender lettuces in the sink,
Wrapping them in cloth to dry.

Burn Your Darlings

What to do with old journals, notebooks
full of the ephemeral and the
profound, words I wrote for an audience—
the high school journal, read biweekly by
Sister Seraphia, and later, things for my eyes only—
when I was suffering from unrequited love, or
loneliness after a clichéd bad breakup—

Dominique advises, *Burn them.* This is what she did, found it
very satisfying. I could burn them one by one in the fireplace. I
could drive them to the summer cottage, in our sandy
backyard, make a bonfire of the journals, watch
them all go in the fire at once, within an hour.

I could take them to a commercial shredding
facility, order the Sheaffer-cartridge-penned pages, the
Pilot razor point-penned sheets sliced thinner than
fennel bulb on a mandoline, sent off to recycling—
I could rip the cover boards off the marble
composition books, use a home shredder machine to
dispatch decades of journals, slowly, one at a time—

The journals are stacked in cardboard boxes in the attic—
I haven't looked at them for years. I don't want
to see what's in them all that anguish, adolescent
introspection, navel-gazing, narcissism of
my twenties. Anything from those times is
lodged somewhere in my brain—if I need to
draw on those experiences for the writing, to impart
a nugget of wisdom to students or my grown children, well—
if I can't remember it, it's gone. Or should be.

I don't want these little burdens, want to
stop holding the paper and all it
records: the perseveration, the romanticism,
the cynicism, the anger, the unanswered
questions, the longing—up in flames, please.

Suze in Midsummer

Not exactly a beauty but you couldn't
take your eyes off her. Dark hair, clear
skin tanned year-round, eyes lined with
kohl. She favored caftans or long
empire waist frocks. In summer, her narrow
feet were encased in Greek sandals, her golden
arms ringed with silver bangles.
Husky-voiced, with an easy laugh, she drew to her
every man in sight. When one of them won her
for a month of two, the rest stepped back,
petitioned to be her friends, would do anything to
stay in that golden orbit.

I used to be heavier, she confessed, but
I owe this—she gestured from slender
neck to painted toenails—to wine,
beer, coffee and—she held
up a tightly rolled joint, slid it
between her lips, accepted a light.

She played a field of unattached males, then at last
settled into domesticity, Upper West Side style,
moved in with a New York radio dj, honey-voiced
like her, only in a deeper register.
She acted off-Broadway, knew where
theater people supped late nights, wove macramé
that found its way into a museum.
Maybe she married the radio guy, lived
happily or not, as so many of us who
married and divorced, not knowing the odds.

I could probably find her now—it's so
easy with the Internet—unless someone wants to
erase herself from the databases, change her name,

win no prizes, publish nothing, refuse to embrace
social media—unless she is not a daughter who
survives her parent, or a sibling—
unless she becomes a non-person online, even if a
somebody to neighbors, coworkers, children,
maybe even grandchildren who point to photos in
old leather-bound albums, asking Glammy, who's
the lady with the dark hair and the bracelets sitting
in the lounge chair, holding the tall frosty glass?

Let me be clear: I don't want to
find Suze, only want to remember that
night at someone's parents' Connecticut house
when they were away. We commandeered the
kitchen, concocted vegetarian salads, opened beers,
bottles of chianti. She watched the men watching
her. I saw it all, her pheromones, her pull on
all of us that midsummer, her laughter spilling
from her to us, overflowing the porches, the deck,
running loose down suburban streets.

Lynne Viti was born and raised in Baltimore, Maryland. She is currently a senior lecturer in the Writing Program at Wellesley College, where for two decades she has taught writing-intensive courses in bioethics, legal studies, media studies, and journalism. A graduate of Mercy High School in Baltimore, she attended the College of Notre Dame of Maryland (now Notre Dame University), and received her B.A. *cum laude* in English Literature from Barnard College. After teaching high school English for several years, she earned her Ph.D. and J.D. from Boston College, where she was a university fellow in English.

After law school, she clerked for the Justices of Superior Court of Massachusetts, and subsequently served as Chief Law Clerk to the Justices. She was an assistant general counsel at the Massachusetts Bay Transportation Authority, where she focused on contracts and appeals work, and later moved to the private sector, working as a litigation associate at a former Boston law firm, Harrison and Maguire, for several years before she resumed her full-time teaching career, at Wellesley College.

Viti has authored numerous academic articles on legal topics, composition theory, literature and media. Her poetry, nonfiction and fiction has appeared in over forty online and print journals and anthologies, including *The Wire: Urban Decay and American Television (2009)*, *The Baltimore Sun*, *Amuse-Bouche*, *The Paterson Review*, *The Little Patuxent Review*, *Drunk Monkeys*, *Cultured Vultures*, *Incandescent Mind*, and *Right Hand Pointing*. She won an Honorable Mention in the 2015 Allen Ginsberg Poetry Contest, and the summer 2015 music poetry contest at *The Song Is*. She blogs at stillinschool.wordpress.com.

CPSIA information can be obtained
at www.ICGtesting.com
Printed in the USA
LVOW13s0310080317
526469LV00010B/86/P